GH00373852

Rhyme and Reason

An Anthology of Poetry

Edited By Amanda Read

δ

Published by Dogma Publications

Dogma Publications, Bicester Innovation Centre, Telford Road
Bicester, Oxon OX26 4LD England

Rhyme and Reason

Anthology Collection © Amanda Read 2005
Copyright © Dogma Publications and Individual Contributors

Cover picture taken from Jan Both's
Ruins at the Sea
Museum of Fine Arts, Budapest

All Rights Reserved

First Published 2005
by Dogma Publications

ISBN 1-84591-010-9

Printed in Great Britain for Dogma Publications

Rhyme and Reason

Contents

Contents Continued

Contents Continued

Restless Earth

Our restless planet shifts and moves,
displays a rage that nothing soothes,
spews out lave, blows out dust,
explodes and jolts the fragile crust.
Furious waves cross oceans, race,
faster, stronger, they gather pace.
Towering walls, they finally crash
on innocent lives, and ruthlessly smash
their way inland. A seething tide,
nowhere to go, no place to hide.
And yet within these tragic waves
there will be some the good Lord saves.
We'll never know why thousands die,
for ours is not to reason why.
But the sleeping giant on which we live
will wake again, and once more give
a mighty roar, a fearsome groan,
and claim the Earth back for his own.

B June V Squires

Ruby

For I lay in bed this winters night gazing at the midnight sky
When I see a gleaming shooting star pass me by
I saw it sparkle like a gem, diamond, or ruby
Talking of rubies one just as special is watching me
But my ruby is very rare and one of a kind
One with a sensitive nature and a kind mind
She may not be here for us to see
With the angels is where she's meant to be
But how I wish she was still down the road
To see the hops of the new spring toad
Oh how she used to love her garden bloom
She used to tidy it like her own bedroom
Nothing out of place but never a mess
She wore her flowery summer dress
Not forgetting her pink marigold gloves
Growing runner beans was her love
Every Sunday she went to the windmill
She had a photograph of it on her windowsill
She told me she wanted to go and see the Queen
She said that but that wasn't the mean
She wanted to see Sandringham House in all the sun
To go in the shops and have a cram bun
But for her it was too far to go
No matter if sun or snow
So I went for her and took a photograph
Of the house, flowers and stone path
She was happy and thankful
She made me gloves made from wool
But she's in heaven now
And I don't know how
But I know she's watching me
And she always will be.

Jemma Walker

A Butterfly Inside Of Me

Inside me something spins a yarn;
Cacophonous, no longer calm.
As if a butterfly within,
Moves, lithe, beneath the layers of skin.

This butterfly inside of me,
Fluttering softly, silently,
Awakens when I think of him;
Starts its dancing and beats its wings.

I see his smile and want to weep;
My butterfly will shrewdly keep
The thought of him inside my heart,
Imprinted there, a tender mark.

His eyes are beauty, flecked with green,
Like butterfly wings rarely seen.
His warmth and humour most of all-
My butterfly adores this jewel.

I know the distance, know how far,
It seems to be to reach this star.
I know he's like a boxed-up gem
Closed off to me; no flower, just stem.

I know that I will never hold,
And feel his heat, or break my cold.
Yet if my mind to such thoughts dives-
It keeps my butterfly alive.

Natasha Liu-Thwaites

Who Benefits?

Summer is gone,
The sky is grey,
Like my life,
Leaves whirl,
On ground bereft of rain,
Through this hot summer,
As I am bereft of love.
Relentlessly my mind asks why?
Why this wanton carnage,
Who benefits from the death
Of my love?
Gunned down in a foreign land
Certainly not I!

Anne M Gibson

Attention

I am waiting here so patiently,
In your garden look and see.
If you do then I shall flee,
Take refuge in the nearest tree.
Preferring distance you from me.

I will always be aloof and shy,
Your greatest friend will not be I
I love the freedom of the sky,
But I must eat, or I shall die.
Thought your garden worth a try.

A birdbath would be so, divine.
Seeds and peanuts will be fine.
Cold winter, is our hardest time
Many friends could die of mine
Cheese, and fats we need to dine.

I will eat worms, some insects too.
Bring my babies you to view
I will always sing a song that's new,
Though I am hungry it is true,
That's all I can do for you.

Alma Hynd

The Long Awaited Return

Long ago, I came from across the sea
I came to seek refuge with your family.
I made a wish to return some day,
And say thanks to you, in some special way.

In the distance I can see,
The same old house that was home to me,
Still painted white with shutters of red,
And my heart quickened as I looked ahead.

There on the porch a familiar figure sat,
Just as I imagined, with her old straw hat,
A little fragile now, with silver in her hair,
Sitting on the porch in her old rocking chair.

The years slipped away as she took my hand,
'Welcome, my child, this is so grand.
Although it has been a very long while,
I remember you still; you have the same smile'.

I walk into the parlour and it felt so good,
To return to the place of my childhood,
We reminisce, about this and that,
And the memories flood back, as we sit and chat.

And the photo albums of long, long ago
Tho' tattered and torn they still can show,
The happy times that passed through those years.
I remember it all and shed a few tears.

I go outside and plant a rose of red,
So it will always be there in her garden bed.
A memory of when, I came back to say,
'Thank you so much', on this special day.

Phillis Green

Sail Away Upon A Dream

Sail away upon a dream,
forgotten, never seen,
sail away upon a dream,
what may, or might, or could have been.

Sail away upon a dream,
upon the ocean blue,
with crimson tides and peaceful shores,
forsaking all that's true.

Sail away upon a dream,
and on, and on, and on,
past floating skies and gleaming stars,
a long lost fable song.

Joanne Alison George

My Only Sister

I feel so cold right now, a frozen feeling within,
I'm a photo frame, with the picture missing.
I crave something with substance,
maybe them crisps that she liked so much,
Or maybe all I really need is her interminable touch.

Feelings, somewhat we shelter,
to realize there's nothing wrong with getting wet,
To rise amongst the crowd,
stuck between heaven and earth, please do not fret.
The thought behind the cards,
a tongue-tied silence is to ear-splitting to take,
If only it was one less candle on my birthday cake.

Being so empty inside, since the first time I cried.
But how can I go on, like bacon on bread, before it is fried.
Is it ok if I go and sit down in the bucketing rain outside?
Cause then you wouldn't have been able to witness how much I cried.

When someone tells you they've experienced the worst pain ever,
They are dead wrong, as I'm sad to say I've had the pleasure of the
pain.
I keep thinking you're going to come down the stairs;
all I can do is stare and stare,
It pains me to think, that you'll never be there,
to embrace me with your heartened care.

Life's harder today than yesterday.
Yet not as hard as it will be tomorrow,
I know you would hate yourself,
for crushing us, in this state of sorrow.
Don't ever feel bad,
you were so precious and should never have to feel down again,
You would do anything to refrain us from going insane.

Surely it's impossible to hurt this greatly,
without as much as a scratch or a graze,
My mind is a maze; you're my only sister
and I will meet you at the other end,
Then I will know if my heart can possibly mend.
You can't be replaced; you can't be disgraced; you're going to fast,
I'll never keep up with you, at such a rapid pace.

With a tender kiss goodbye, I await the day our family re-unites,
Then we can have some more of them good old family unit fights.
I can do anything now;
I've already done the hardest thing I could possibly carry out,
Thank-you for that Sis,
I'll be ready for any card that life intends to be dealt.

Please recognize how much I love you;
your name will constantly be an imprinted tattoo,
I'll see you once more Sister, when my life is through.

Joseph Scarrott

The Homecoming

We've been away,
just a short stay
to get a well earned break.

All does look well,
But who can tell
what calamities await us.

What will we find?
For we left behind
four loveable grown-up boys.

The roses full blown,
The grass has grown
Too much to hope they'd cut it?

The door's ajar-
They can't be far
but not a soul in sight.

We start to worry,
get in a flurry
in case we have been burgled.

But all is well
for one can tell,
no signs of an intruder.

Left in the sink
filled to the brink
unwashed dishes, enough for a week!

Clothes on the floor,
washing galore
an muddy footprints through the hall.

Beds in a mess,
Oh, what a mess
a large family engenders.
We love them really,
really dearly,
but they could have a little more thought.

But, joy of joys,
Boys will be boys.
How dull life would be without them.

Beryl Stone

Our Lodger

Sid lives here
We don't know where
He's in the kitchen
And up the stairs
He does all the things
That we don't do
When things are quiet
We know he is too
But take care, things
Will happen
When we are unaware
So be on your guard
And beware
Sid is cunning
And we are gunning
So look out Sid
We are coming.

Enid Cowdrey

March 4th 2005

On March 4th, oh! What a day.
Every weather came our way
We started out with heavy snow.
Then sun came out to make it go.
And while out shopping it turned to rain.
Then sleet, and hail, and snow again.
In the car I sat to wait.
To hope this deluge would abate.
Eventually I went indoors.
To what I thought we loud applause.
I stopped to listen to this sound.
Yes, it was thunder rumbling round.
I didn't venture out again.
Yes you guessed, more snow and rain.
In 65 years of my life altogether.
I've not seen this, in one days weather.

Doreen Simmonds

We're Two Of A Kind

Wake up early morning come rain or shine,
Then wake up our owners around about nine.
Then off to the park where we can have a good run,
We go after the same stick, oh what fun.

We love the park where we meet all our friends,
People think we look like a pair of bookends.
Go to obedience classes that's why we're so good.
But sometimes get carried away and end up in the mud.

So when we get home we stink out the front room,
Time for a bath and a jolly good groom.
We've won a few shows we like to show off,
Our owners we love, but we cost them a lot.

We have to be trimmed, as our fur does not shed,
Can't see through the hair that we have on our head.
Have you guessed the dogs that we could be?
We're a pair of Wheaten's called Mabel and Betsy.

Brenda Wedge

My Love

Please don't ever doubt my love
For its strength will never fade
But instead it grows stronger
My love for you will never age
And please don't let me hear you say
Why are you with me here today
For foolish words
Make me feel so sad
For you're the best thing in life
I've ever had
So never doubt and never ponder
Just believe me and never wonder
For this is now and we are one
And every day I see the sun
The golden sun and you by my side
Make me feel so happy
And warm inside. X

Pauline Green

Ships

When I was young and innocent
And hope flowed swift in me,
I'd wander slowly across the shore
And gaze far out to sea.

Sometimes a distant ship sailed by,
It's route a far off land,
And then my dreams ignited
And hatched upon the sand.

My heart swelled with emotion
For all that was to come.
Before me stretched a magic path
And I was poised to run.

Now as I filter through my life
And muse on all I've seen,
I care not where the ships are bound,
But wonder where they've been.

Christine Smith

The Wind

I have the hunger of a thousand winds
Am beckoning you on to see my soul
You ignite me with your thoughts of emotion
Of desire for others
But don't get to close!
For I am the wind that could blow you out.
Never fear! I mean you no harm, for I am not real,
I have no face, body or voice,
I only have a presences that only you can feel.
For I am not real, am only the gentle
Summers breeze blowing on your face.
It's just a small reminder that I am still here,
For I am still your soul mate from now and forever
So don't be sad
I didn't leave, for I am still here, walking at your side
For I am the genteel summers breeze,
Rustling at the leaves on a bright summers day.

Nicola Wood

Pride

Sleek, brown-haired girl
in jeans, low slung, hips tilted
hangs around astro-turf
watching adolescents
pant and trash
the length and breath.

Fifteen, twenty minutes
undeterred she waits
in sultry expectation.
To see and to be seen,
a mark of love's sweet care.

Jangling chain-linked fence
sounds the hour's end
sending sweaty airtex lurching
north, south and due east.

A greeting, a further exchange
then clumsy words like phantom
clods from muddied boots
fall dampening her resonance.

The car revs,
the horn sounds
but two fingers held aloft
decline the ride.

Claire M Buckland

Mother Of The Groom

Mike and Sarah are to be wed,
The gold embossed invitation said,
At St. Luke's Church at two o'clock,
I'll have to go out and choose a new frock.

What do think to this big hat?
Does this dress make me look too fat?
What about the bag and shoes?
I don't want to look like yesterdays news.

I want my son to be proud of his Mum,
Is this too tight across the bum?
Does the jacket reach my thigh?
Are these heels a bit too high?

No, I don't like that dark green,
It's the worst I've ever seen,
And as for that in brightest yellow,
I want something much more mellow.

This is too short it looks all wrong,
And that one there is much too long.
What about this one here in blue?
I'll look good in that standing next to you.

So here we are on the happy day,
I'm feeling good I have to say,
But I'll stand over here, a bit to one side,
Everyone's looking at the beautiful bride.

Joan L Defraine

Touching The Blue

hurt pain red raw
words stick closed craw
envy seethed opal green
eyes shocked vivid scene
spine yellow tinged
fear inward cringed
heart deepest black
walls pressure crack
reach out pursue
touching the blue

Steve Mann

Euthanasia

Locked in a cell, I have lost the key
My feelings are stuck, will never be free
My jail my body both lifeless and still
Wanting to die commit suicide, self kill.

I long for movement I long for touch
I long for my eyesight but it's all too much
For my body to take it rots everyday
Until I wilt like a flower while for death I do pray..

I am trying my hardest to get out of my state
Not eating or drinking yet they keep me awake
Force fed through a tube I cannot detach
Made to live when the train to death I wish I could catch

Why live when all I can do is sleep?
I am like a cadaver living dead so I weep
I cannot tell them, yet I scream inside
Until my voice box bleeds, yet I'm still pushed aside.

So give me that pistol, give me a knife
Give me an injection to end this broken down life
Put something in my food, drown me while I sleep
I don't care how you do it I must die to release what is skin deep.

I can't be happy while I suffer in silence
I am calm on the outside yet my inside feels violence
So lay me to rest let me now cry in peace
Hear my plea to be dead and let my suffering cease.

Robert John Slade

Communion

The child in me sees
The child in you.

The woman in me feels
The man in you.

The spirit in me loves
The spirit in you.

The soul in me knows
The soul in you.

Judith Kelman

I'm Still Me

I'm young, I'm free, I'm so alive,
I drink, I smoke, I sleep away,
I never worry I take no care,
I live with danger I like to play,
But recently, I've begun to slow,
Twenty-three, yet I've lost my glow,
Out last night, I fclt uneasy,
My body unresponsive, tired and weak.

I couldn't go to work today,
I don't feel young, nor free, or alive,
I can't hold my drink, smoke, sleep away?
I've lost my will, can't live to the challenge,
I've stepped into a chasm, and I can't break free,
Now I worry, I'm afraid to play,
I've seen the danger I know the fear,
I have no strength; it's no longer here.

I'm in the hospital, all alone,
The doctor he stares, he holds the news,
I don't feel strong, yet I have to cope,
'HIV' he mumbles, but his eyes betray,
What it is, that he is wanting to say,
However, then he takes me by the hand,
He knows the pain, the hurt, the sorrow,
And I know, he'll still be there for me tomorrow,
It's then he speaks, his heart so true,
'Where there's love, there's hope for you'.

So I'm still young, still free, and alive,
I still drink, smoke, enjoy my day,
I try not to worry, and I take the right care,
I'm HIV, but do you know what? I'm still there.

Peter Morris-Webb

Pippy Head

March, march, march
Up and down feet of nonsense
Eleventy toes with minds of their own
Socks are banished from the Owen toe
Marching, marching, marching.

Ian Bale

You Love Me Too!

You have restored hope in my heart,
I don't want this love to fall apart,
Boy I love you; you know it's true,
And no matter what I always will do.

You've told me you feel the same,
So please don't play me like a game,
Cos I don't think my heart can take anymore,
It's been hurt so many times before.

So take my hand let me know that you're mine,
Then I know that we'll be fine,
Cos you know that I love you
And I know that you love me too!

Dawn Coser

My Son

My son you've grown to be a man
My pride is there to see,
For all the things you have become
And all yet still to be.

I know that you don't need me now
In ways you did before
But still I know that deep within
You hold an open door.

I wish I could protect you
From all that is not good,
But life and fate deal out the cards
And that's the way they should.

So in the quiet of the night
I say a silent prayer
That God will keep you in his sight
And ever in his care.

Barbara Robinson

Spotted Dick

Now here's a tale of spotted Dick,
Who'd no unusual fetishes,
Except just one - he'd call by name
His ugly spots and blemishes.

Developing a carbuncle,
He said, 'I'm sure this spot'll
Match the one Onassis had,
So I'll call it Aristotle!'

And when four nasty yellow heads
Erupted in a cluster,
And burst together with a pop,
He named the area, Buster!

Then once, when playing tennis
He developed two big blisters
Which ruined his game, they very soon
Became the Williams sisters!

And when two groups of pustules grew
To form a virtual war zone,
He designated one group, Westlife,
The other he called, Boyzone!

But the blemish he's most proud of
Bar a nobble on his right knee,
Is a small protuberance on his thumb,
A wart, which he calls Disney!

Tony Reese

A Field Of Daisies

The yellow daisy free and bright,
Not cultivated to be,
But, they are the best
Just to shine to your delight
Like a pearl in a net
Always to be,
Greatly admired
A shooting star
Then fell and lay
And gently swaying around
And flowering on a
Summer's day.

A free, a happy jewel
Yellow inspired
More happy than the
Rural singing of a skylark
As the daylight fades
Away into the dark.

Sammy Michael Davis

If I Tell You That I Love You

If I tell you that I love you.
If I promise that I care.
Will it bridge this gap between us
or will I always have to share?

If I say your mine forever.
If I say there's no one else.
Will it close this gap between us?
If I lie it's to my-self.

It's in your eyes
I know you love me.
It's in your touch
I know you care.
No, I'll never close this gap between us.
I know I'll always have to share.

Jennifer Miller

Life Is Just An Act

I've become an actor, acting out my life
Always playing solo roles, the broken hearted wife

Sometimes my part is happy and sometimes just plain sad
To see the roles that others have and some I wish I had

Sometimes my part is well rehearsed I play it to its best
Another time it's not so good, I'm really put to the test.

Sometimes I play a leading role, but then there is no choice
No one to share decisions, its but a single voice.

Sometimes I've taken such a role I've even been applauded
But acting is just but an art, an art I've been afforded

Sometimes it's just a walk on part, I wouldn't ask for me
Longer in the dressing room, the comfort of closed doors.

Sometimes I play a family role they're fun and full of life
But the role I always yearn for is the one called husband and wife.

Ann Best

Within Our Heads

Within the boundaries of our head
A light year leaps and is lost instead
Of filling a space as large as thought
And the spanner of space spins and is caught
In webs of wonderous light and shade
And moves toward what the maker made.

So reaching out ahead of time
Gives man in thought, careless of rhyme
Or reason for going there at all
When stars and suns begin to fall
And the secret in the findings fails
To leave its finder nought but wails
However far our ships must sail
It's within our heads that we must hail
The truth of all that we have and need
To greet the sun with a planted seed.

Maurice Bagley

Stop - Think

Where are all the kind-hearted people who used to live on Earth,
are they the only ones who have but gone in death?
There seems to be no mercy in this world of ours,
so many senseless killings in each and every hour.
We read of stupid bombings, of wrecking homes and pubs.
Please tell me - if you can - is it done by senseless cubs?
The innocent always suffer, no matter what the 'cause'
so I challenge these senseless people to take time - pause.
Think of your innocent victims - killed - maimed - blind
What harm have they done you? They too are your mankind
Take time to look around you, tell me what you see.
You must know by now everyone is cursing thee.
Are all your kind who cause this pain
Like yourself - senseless and insane?

Grace Hoggan

The Mark

You made this mark on my skin
You made your mark on everything
I tore this wound on to my flesh
You're the reason my life's a mess
I'm ending my life just to forget
The way you left me with out regret
The blood is flowing from my wrist
My life is over will I be missed?

Ian Price

Sally's Adventure

One hot day on her way home from school,
Sally went swimming to try and keep cool.
The river in flood after torrents of rain,
To keep swimming, poor Sally, was always in vain
She struggled, dear Sally, the bank to regain,
But couldn't and Sally screamed 'gain and again.
Her cries were heard by a farmer nearby
Who was harvesting there in a field full of rye.
He sprang to the rescue in a moment of haste,
And dived into the river, stripped to the waist.
Sally was frantic and very soon sank,
Then the man reached for her and strove for the bank.
The river was raging and the man was near spent,
And farmer and girl, with the current they went.
Then the two of them saw a tree overhung,
And with one might effort the farmer he clung,
Sally reached up and caught hold of the bough,
'Go make for the bank,' the man yelled; 'now, now, now'.
Sally edged slowly and carefully along,
Praying that she would do nothing wrong.
She reached the bank and dropped to the ground
Then taking a breath, she arose and looked round.
The farmer soon followed her to the bank
Sally tottered towards him and gave him her thanks.
'You'd better come home,' said the man, 'meet the wife
have a hot bath, and thank God for your life!'
Thus ends the tale of Sally's adventure,
And the promise she made that she'd no longer venture.
Alone to the river, no matter how calm,
To give mother and father a cause for alarm.

Bernard J Webster

Dreams Of Yesterday

Our dreams of yesterday passed us by,
We did but give life our said try,
Dreams are in that of our own head,
Many come to pass it is so said,
We all have dreams of what's to be,
Many of them we never do see,
Dreams of the living in times to be,
In our dreams this we all wish to see,
But what of the dreams, those of the night,
Many of them just keep out of sight,
We all dream in many the way,
In our dreams having our own say,
Dreams do at times come then to be,
But not in the ways we them do see,
In dreams we look for the easy way out,
The sorting out of our lives to be brought about,
Life is not like that at any one time,
This life to live is that of yours and mine,
To dream is theirs, a fool at the heart,
With the life having they would so part,
Yet that life for them was so meant to be,
The soul not tied but to be so free,
Indulge we can in that of our own dream,
In this of living you may not be so keen,
A dream is a thought in that of its making,
At sometimes in life you will be part of its taking,
On you it could but turn around and about,
Another's dream could have the last shout.

June Annie Davis

Life's Trials And Tribulations

The memories of times gone by
The happy times of past
Some will always be there
And some will never last

Life's trials and tribulations
Are with you throughout your life
Whether it's having kids
Or marrying a wife

Things are sent to try us
Sometimes we can get low
You feel that you can't cope any more
And there's nowhere to go

Life's trials and tribulations
Don't think you can get by
For help, you only need to ask
Don't let the chance walk by

When you're feeling low one day
Just sitting round to mope
Think of those great memories
To help you get by and cope

Life's trials and tribulations
Not happiness and wealth
Remember all the happy times
At least you're in good health

Dave Boyce

Lost Love

I remember the day of our first kiss
A couple of beats my heart did miss
The shivers up and down my spine
Is another thing that springs to mind.

As time passed by things got better
A single red rose and even a letter
Phone calls came every single day
Saying you loved me in every way.

Now the phone doesn't ring anymore
You don't come calling at my door
I wish you had the courage to say
That the time had come to call it a day.

Now our relationship has reached an end
And the love we had will never mend
I'm afraid that love has gone forever
Away to the land of never, never.

Ann Turner

Little Old Me

I thought, I would write a letter today
I am all prepared with nothing to say.
My head is buzzing the words are there
But all I can do is sit here and stare-
So I went to the kitchen and made some tea
But there's no one to share it with little old me.

How many people are out there and cold?
The lonely, the outcasts and the very old.
As time passes by with nowhere to go
I look at the clock and that is slow.
Has time stood still at half past three?
No one cares for little old me.

The days are lonely the nights are long
Oh how I wish for my loved one gone.
But I know one day we shall meet again-
Perhaps the sun will shine or there may be rain,
But when my eyes are dim and I'm eighty-three
At last, there will be someone to take care of me.

Miriam Lloyd

Life

We wander by because they are free
The lovely leaves that form a tree
Flowers with heavenly scent and hue
Are scarcely noticed by me and you.

Songs of the birds that greet the dawn
Makes us happy and our hearts warm
Sunshine that gives the earth good cheer
Brings memories of love - not fear.

True appreciation is a gift so rare
That many men and women are not aware
That help is such a splendid deed
Which brings comfort to those in need.

Familiarity dulls ones perception
And often causes painful deception
Selfish people have an endless groan
Happiness is not a virtue-they own.

Life is what you make it, so let laughter sing
With deep affection and the sunshine bring
Good fortune, good health and happiness galore,
To arrive this day and remain for evermore.

God gave us flowers and birds
The grazing cattle in herds
Mountain, moorland and leas
God's gift the world over - to please.

Claude Taylor

In Whose Company

Content in the presence of whose lips upturned
Whilst drowning in such seldom summer rays
And whose bird-song from lips, sometimes for days
Recites philosophies, by others spurned?
Content in the breeze of whose swift movement
As olfactory sense is heightened for hours,
Not sated by the scent of wild spring flowers
Yet vexed, by whose aromatic raiment?
But whose fragile heart can be sorely torn,
Impaled upon words uncouth and cruel
From the shallow depths of a mindless fool?
In their side, your Hindustani soul, a thorn
And in my own…a stigmata of love;
Content, I praise you and the Lord above.

Stephen Michael McGowan

The Jar Of Marmalade

We have it every breakfast time
(It's some unwritten rule)
The colour always cheers me up
Before I go to school.

We're just a fair-sized family
With Mum and Dad and me;
There's brother Jack who goes to work
And Linda, only three.

Mum serves oats, then eggy course
It's scrum but quite a bore
For what I want comes at the end -
The stuff that I adore.

The others like it too, you know,
Though take it in their stride,
But Linda's sitting up on high
Her mouth is open wide...

She snatches for the sticky mass
She simply loves the taste
And now it's all around her chin!
Oh what a dreadful waste!

Dad takes just a moderate bit
And passes it to Mum,
And then it goes to brother Jack -
My turn will never come!

Oh boy! Oh Boy! It's on its way
It can't be long delayed...
I'll dig into that simply gorgeous
Jar of Marmalade.

Peggy Hovell

Walk On Water

Though I can walk on water
I just can't break the ice
I need to make my mind up
I need to take my own advice
I search for words of wisdom
Though they should come from me
I'm trapped inside these feelings
With no escape that I can see.

I step into this nightmare
When we come face to face
Where all my deepest thoughts are frozen
All my intentions lost in space
Although these words are flowing
It's easy when I'm on my own
But when at last I make my mind up
I turn around and you are gone.

Terry Pratley

Stress Relief

A throbbing in the groin, a flush of pink to the face
  A deep intake of breath, passionately cool like Nottingham Lace.
Heartbeat pulsating, becoming faster with time,
  Juices turning to acid, like an erotic green lime.
A paltry sound is uttered – a squeak of ecstasy,
  Soon to be followed by what is begged to be
A resounding, deep tormenting moan
  Becoming lustful in its dulcet tone.
Herculean urge engulfs the pace
  As it magnifies across his face.
The heat, it sizzles, crackling wild,
  No time to be coy, or meek or mild.
Inhibitions forgotten of mortal mind,
  Passions conceived from stress of a kind.
Explosive embrace of the other so strong
  Emanating for seconds, yet feeling so long.
Stroking of erogenous zones
  Blood firing all angles round skeletal bones.
His flamboyant penis erect with pride,
  She grabs him, he enters her deep and wide.
An aroma of roasting, grinding as one
  Like coffee beans when matured in the sun.
The smell of lust lays heavy in the air
  They come together, but do they care?
Like Nazis of torture, they do not stop
  'Til they can take no more and are fit to drop.
As the moon now glows bright, high in the sky
  Angst ebbed and flowed away…it has died.
A warm glow of embers are felt inside
  Both bodies refreshed, stress turned with the tide.

Alison Sutton

Energy

We share holy fire
And tiger bright nights.

We recite poems
In the fields of our homelands.

We make love
In the graveyards of our ancestors.

We drink traditional liquor
In the parks of our neighbourhoods.

We hitchhike
In the dangerous cars of our country.

We sleep
In the strange beds of our women.

We share holy fire
In the tiger bright nights of our wild Africa.

Lee Richard Kirsten

A.M. Blues

I wake up every morning and get out of bed
Sometimes I find I'm wishing I could snuggle down instead
But the habits of a lifetime are always hard to break
I'm programmed to a set routine with far too much at stake
So it's straight into the bathroom, a quick look at my face
With its bleary eyes and whiskers I feel it's a disgrace
But there's not much I can do to alter natures line
Just shave and freshen up a bit and pretend I'm feeling fine
From there into the kitchen where I fill the well used kettle
I'm feeling slightly better now but still not on my mettle
A slice of toast, a cup of tea and I'm ready for the fray
The only trouble is it's the same damn thing each day
I even stopped the paper 'cos I felt it cost too much
Now I must admit I miss it for it helped me keep in touch
Instead I've got my radio my constant vocal friend
Without it I really think I'd go clean round the bend
It gives out things called time checks to make sure we're not late
So on the dot of eight o' clock I'm out the garden gate
Unlock the car and turn the key and start out on the drive
And get to work by five to nine it's the time we all arrive
At half pest ten its coffee and at one o' clock its lunch
Have you ever stopped to wonder why we're such a routine bunch
Tea at three and leave at six and home again at seven
Prepare a meal, watch the 'box' and in bed by eleven
Another day is over, another day is done
And in another eight hours time I'll start another one!

Tony Wright

Newbiggin Ladies

Haul away! Haul away! Keep the carriage running free
Get the AUGUSTUS and Laura down to the sea,
Haul away! Ladies, with a resolute smile
Haul along PANT ROAD, then nearly a mile
O'er the heathland and moor, and doon the 'Ashby Gutter'
With quickening heart, giving many a flutter.
Haul away! Ladies, haul handsomely
To the WHITEHOUSE SKEARS, then we'll see
The AUGUSTUS and LAURA floating free
Saving the EMINENT crew from a cruel sea.
So Haul away! Ladies, a launching we'll see
By the Launching Ladies of Newbiggin-by-the Sea.

There's Val, Irenie, Susan and Jane
Catherine and Jeannie, June and Elaine
There's Belle and Betty, Helen and Claire
Liza and Lizzie, and the Robinson Pair
There's Dora and Doreen, Maggie and May
Christine and Chrissie, Ruby and Fay.
There's Margaret and Maureen, Alice and Dot
Melissa and Ivy, Jennifer and Tot.
There's Ina O'Brien and her daughter Annie
Kitty and Janet, Louisa and Nannie.

So Haul away! Haul away! Keep the carriage running free
Haul away! Ladies, now handsomely
Haul away! Ladies, Haul resolutely
Slip the AUGUSTUS and LAURA, float her free
Launched by the Ladies of Newbiggin-by-the Sea.
So Haul away! Haul away!, a launching we'll see
By the Launching Ladies of Newbiggin-by-the Sea.

Andrew Quinn

Global Warming

Four billion years this earth has spun
And yearly tracked around the sun.
Four billion years to cool and form
And battered by the meteors storm
To shape the earth and fill the seas
To raise the mountains and the trees
And simple life its roots to take
And ultimately great apes make.

A thousand times the climate altered
And species died and leaders faltered
The trilobite, the dinosaur
Who once were king but now no more
The message that the fossil sends
Tells of changes and dead ends
But man thinks only with conceit
That nature he can tame and beat.

Now global warming we are told
Will make us hot, or makes us cold.
Will brings us floods, or bring us drought.
Will change the seasons without doubt.
And make the waters quickly rise
Or disappear before our eyes.
Will herald in a new Ice Age
Or scorching sun and desert rage.

Our puny race , a microcosm,
The smallest trace in Gaia's bossum.
Yet still we cannot comprehend
The mammals age sometime will end
And in five billion years or so
The sun will blossom and will grow.
Consume the earth with cosmic fury
And none will hear about our story

David Wilkinson

The Earth Moved

The Earth moved, the World shook,
Life changed forever,
Loved ones lost,
Family's torn apart,
People never to be seen again,
The World is different,
We are different,
The Earth moved,
Our hearts moved,
We want to help,
But, how will it ever be enough?

Lucy Beams

From Birth To Death

Who really knows
what our lives will be
when they cut the cord
that sets us free
No one can share
that moment in time
with the whole world before us
do we think 'it's mine!'

We take take take for
the next few years
with people around us
to allay our fears
Out into the world
we bravely go
So much to do, those
wild seeds to sow!

As our minds become slower
and our bodies frail
there's no one to help us
when our tired hearts fail
We've been through it all
and would do again
But why didn't I? I wish!
would be our refrain

Rowena Haley

Trust

Such high hopes had I for our love
In you I put all my trust
Family and friends I cast aside
In you I had such pride.

Never a word did I doubt
Of all the things you talked about
And when on my finger the ring you set
I blessed the day that we had met
My love for you knew no bounds
For the happiness that I had found.

Now alas, my trust is shattered
All my plans now are scattered
For I have just discovered
That you belong to another
And on you I have no claim
as another bears your name.

I must cast you from my life
Knowing I never can be your wife
My pride is hurt
My trust is gone
In my heart there is no song.

Time will heal I have no doubt
But for now I want to shout
How could you have been so unkind
Knowing that you told such lies?

Trissie Burgess

Life Is So Precious

The day when I was told those dreaded words,
'You have breast cancer' I felt so scared.
My whole life passed me by I was struck dumb,
I didn't hear a word that was said to me I felt so numb.
All the things they told me I didn't understand
I was so shocked at the time my daughter holding my hand.
I remember when she took me home it was a clear as day
I was haunted by the word cancer it just wouldn't go away
Being so very upset I just wanted to shout
Couldn't wait for my treatment I just wanted the cancer out.
All my family were supportive, they also were in shock
My husband standing by me, he was my rock.
It's been a while now; it has felt like a dream
There isn't a day goes by, thinking what could have been.
I think I have got a guardian angel watching over me
As I got through my illness I felt it was meant to be.
I started thinking positive and that's what pulled me through
With out the love of my friends and family I don't know what I'd do.
We've only got one life, I'm sure you would agree too.
We must live it to the full, that's what it has made me do.

Barbara Jackson

Scotland Arise!

Scotland's our future and our hope,
It binds us to our roots,
In years to come we'll honour all
And strive to nurture shoots.

All people here in this proud land
Can help to lead us clear,
from grief and strife and poverty,
Pain hunger, shame and fear.

A caring, prosperous home to build
That'll surely be our claim,
To Scotland's past we'll look again
To guide us to our aim.

Old Scotia can, in this new world,
Stand proud and straight and true,
To be a trusted friend to all
Our foibles to eschew

Ian Saint-Yves

If We Knew

If we knew that this life that we have is all that we have.
Would we become
more selfish,
selfish in being
happier,
selfish in not caring
about anything,
but to be happy,
but to understand,
but to forgive,
others
for not knowing
that
this life that we have
is all that we have.

Sue Sharpe

Web Sight

September spider spins her web
Of gossamer and gold;
But woe betide each moth or fly
Its sticky threads enfold.
A web looks such a fragile thing
Yet still the wind it rides,
Well-anchored to a swaying bush
The spider-queen bestrides.
Her web it is both fine and strong
So neat in ev'ry line;
And when it's decked in morning dew
And sunshine - it's divine!

Jim Lawes

Puzzling Ways

Another day
Another way
Forever hoping for you
To have your say.
What have I said
That worried your head
What have I done,
That you stay so dumb.
Silence is golden
Again it is said,
Doors maybe open.
Barriers made to be broken
A genuine shake of the hand
To help you to expand
Then to relax.
Wherever you are or ever may be
I want you to know
You are always with me.
But to haunt I will not, because
I love you lots. A token never to be broken

Edith Blagrove

Dying High

All I ever want to be
Crawling far ahead of me
Calling deep within to me
Murdering my soul.

Never mind the bumblebees
Before you, down onto their knees
Living in the empty breeze
Soaked in rock 'n' roll.

Push away the butterflies
Of long forgotten neon nights
No one cares and no one tries
Fighting to live on.

If you don't have it you don't win
Give up; don't try to be like him
Just because you could've been
Following the Sun.

Mickayla Dawes

The Gate

The fear of walking out the gate is one I can't explain,
It rises from the stomach, an invisible, choking pain.
You can feel the joy beneath it, fighting to struggle out,
Confusion mixed with disbelief and a craving just to shout!

What will I find beyond that fence now that the time has come?
I'm proud of my achievement, now my sentence time is done.
But deep inside a bubbling shame of the wrong doings in the past,
The knowledge of the grief and woe on so many, I have cast.

But out of all the evil that I've witnessed every week,
The attitude, the senseless acts that on drugs,
the 'smack-heads' wreck.
For 12 long months my eyes
have seen the animals that walked the streets,
The boasting and the banter of 'their heroic, criminal feats!'

So here we are – it's eight o clock one last look round my room,
And as I walk across The Square I can feel a pang of gloom.
A couple of mates who have to stay,
thumbs raised and nodding heads,
To see one walk to freedom, I know tears them to shreds.

And at the gate, just one last glance to what has been my home,
It certainly reached my inner sense, the guilt of what I'd done.
Will any-body listen if I tell them of my fate?
Because they certainly didn't bother on the inside of that gate!

Robert Brooker

The Heart

The emotions
    Of the heart
        Should never
            Be questioned...

For it has
    A mind
        Of it's
            Own...

Laura Lamarca

When I Was Young

Shrimps and winkles for Sunday tea
The muffin man would always be
Ringing his bell with all his might
And the hot chestnut man warmed up the night
Toasting forks, hot buttered toast
All sitting down to the Sunday roast
Bellows pumping, arms aching,
Making sure the bread is baking
Hard boiled eggs with hand painted faces
Roll them downhill, everyone chases
Come Halloween, apples in barrels floating
Hideous masks with faces gloating
Pumpkins, with features that shine
Jacket potatoes and hot ginger wine
Christmas pudding, sixpence hidden
Taste of mix strictly forbidden
Real holly, home made decorations
Christmas evening visit friends and relations
For colds, flu, or even the croup
Mums magic cure was onion soup
Whips and tops, wooden hoops
Tin soldier armies, I controlled the troops
Hopscotch, five stones, marbles to play
No television to watch all day
The man with the cart totting for rags
Exchanging for goldfish in water filled bags
Wartime over, things looking up
Charlton even won the FA cup
It doesn't seem so long ago
But counting the years, it is you know.

Calvin White

A Grey Cloud

A grey cloud descended on us, not sent from heaven or hell,
But from the borough council and it has an awful smell.

The odour is obnoxious and its one I've smelt before,
Greed, its on the deadly sin list, the one that makes me poor.

To cap it all those men up there from my misery take credit.
'Come on sir, its not so bad you can pay by direct debit'.

'You know you can afford it and looking at it all in all
It will make your telephone bill seem so very small'.

Council tax I hate you, more than MOT's or VAT,
I need to vent my frustration, and I'm quite fond of our old cat.

You guys must think I'm loaded, but money rather sparse,
So keep your council tax demand, because it really is a farce.

Ivor Griffiths

Realisation

Yes, it hurts to realise,
After all these years of lows and highs,
Of fears and worry and feeling bad,
Spending my life, feeling so sad!

I've often wondered why I'm here,
'Cause life's been a living hell,
With people treating me so cruel,
And, ME taking it so well.

I've discovered, I DO count,
After I've been MADE to feel,
A pest, a joke, not worth a light,
And trodden under heel.

The last few weeks I've found myself,
Amongst the OTHER side,
The days are gone of feeling worst,
I'm so happy I could burst!

I have found so many friends,
FAR worse off than me,
They've taken ME into their lives,
And given me company.

So anything that's happened before,
That's dragged me down so far,
I'm leaving behind, on the ground,
And moving up a floor!

Marion Doherty

The Equalizer

Prizes for all losers
And relief from ears of ringing
And for folk with skin disease
I'd like to stop their toes from stinging
Little boys with broken toys
Move aside I'll fix it
For hungry dogs I'd like to make the
Never ending biscuit.

Antony Hateley

When War Is Done
(Written to Katherine Sherlock Sept 42-45)

Some day, my darling, the sun will break through, Behold!
To reveal a sweet picture of you
I walk out to greet you, my love all afire
And kiss you, my darling the wife I admire
And as the clouds break and the sun reappears
Your face I shall see with your eyes full of tears
They'll stand not for sorrow, or heartaches
or woe or for the time that your lover did go
they'll be tears of great joy, your heart beating fast
Yes, see me my darling, I've come home at last
I answered the call and my time I have done
And now I return, to you and our son
No more shall I venture to leave home sweet home
Or have some one tell me, this country you'll roam.
I've come back to live, to be honest and true
To build up my home, yes, my darling, with you.
So now let us live through the years to the end
Until God does call up and we turn the bend.

George Sherlock

Chained Melody

A soft breath of air
Pauses to caress her lips
Loses faith and leaves.

The slack lips opened
In licked anticipation
To receive the kiss.

In a leap of faith
The fantasy becomes real
Anticipation.

A moment of lust
Lost in the temple of dreams
Becomes obsolute.

As faith leaves the day
The dreaming spire rises to sing
Rhapsody in blue.

Blue moon stalks the night
Stealing into the shadows
Bathes her lonely room.

Another day done
She picks up her knitting wool
And strokes her small cat.

Marjorie Nye

Night-time Thoughts

Where have all the places gone?
All I have is memories to hold.

Scattered friends
Where are you when I need you?

Deserted and alone
I feel the breeze.
Do you feel it too?

My final cigarette
Even you know the end is near.

Sleep is all that contains me
Hopes and fear collect at my feet.

I will see them in the morning
When daylight breathes through my window.

The dawning of a new day.
Am I ready for you?

Ellen Jones

I Want My Dreams

Break the looking glass
It gives a better effect when shattered
Like my dreams
That none have seen
Crumble with hopes rotting hand
Lost to eyes that harken to my demise
A pretty to burn all convictions
Lay it in my youthly hand
For the plague is contained in the mind
A wretched dark space of grimace
Allow me to strike the match
Watch it tumble
As I stumble to redefine my reasons for action
Breathless sense as flame settles in kindling
The empty hole inside returns
Now exhale as knees find the dirt
Hands tear at dyed roots
Sky spiral of burning flame an intoxication
Eyes tear the open vision to darkness
Eternal ire an expression
Of throat made clear
Nothing left to fear as eye silver fails to rage
I want my dreams

Sophie Petrie

A Lost Love

My heart will always miss a beat
when I see someone on the street
that reminds me of you.

I will always seek your face in an empty room
when the music plays it will be you whispering
the words and making the notes a melody.

It was a time when two people loved each other
and the world stood still.

Dawn Morris

Moonlight

I watch from the outside as we share a kiss
my mind carried to another plane by passion,
with an enraptured embrace I hold you tight
two hearts racing as we dance in the moonlight,
your body against mine as we become one
an enriched union of common delight filling us,
enchanted souls by love labours wrought
a pairing to last as long as time and beyond.

Amy Culpepper

Childlike

We walked round the Zoo
Till our feet were sore and ached.
We stopped by the monkeys' cage,

We stared; he looked to be in a rage.
He was having none of it,
These folks, who just come to see,

So, looking over his shoulder at me;
He turned round to show us
His big red bare bum…see

I looked at young Michael
And he looked at me, Hey! Is he blushing?
Or did it happen through drinking his tea'.

I looked at Michael and wanted to laugh,
And he looked at me.
I got serious now and said,
Are you considering at all, that he might be a she?

Kathleen Bartholomew

Family Life

To belong to a loving family
is life's greatest treasure
To share our joys and our sorrows too
Is something beyond measure.

To give and take
is the rule of the game
To bear each others burdens
And to keep ones hopes aflame.

Love is the thing that binds us together
And will withstand, whatever the weather
For only when life's storms are passed
Shall we find the calm that will surely last.

One can't imagine what life would be
Without a loving family
So if you experience these things too
Grasp with both hands - as others do.

For it may be the envy of many a soul
Who do not to such belong
So set an example-and grateful be
And let love be nurtured and strong.

Remember, a sense of belonging surpasses all
Far better than being alone
So take heart therefore and let love grow
For there is no place like home.

Gillian Morgan

100 Miles

A hundred miles of poetry, is what I tend to do,
It keeps my mind from wandering, or else I think of you.
Which as I get further from you, feels my soul with dread,
The thought of how I left you, alone asleep in bed.

My heart tells me to turn around and head back to your door,
And to feel the gentle touch of you, like all those times before.
Though you are just wonderful and I really do love you,
I know I have got no choice, it's what I have to do.

So the scenery I don't notice, as I keep driving past,
And I think of our life together and the fate that has been cast.
Each Minute that I travel, makes the pain just more intense,
As Mile by every mile, the distance grows immense.

But soon I'll be at my destination, I'm sure I won't be late,
In another fifteen minutes, I will be driving through the gate.
And I will endure the eight hours, as I do so many days,
But when they are over, I'll be back upon my way,

This time I am so happy, I wear a joyous coat,
As I head back towards you, from my 100 mile commute.

Stuart C Rogers

Scarlet Ribbon

Take my hand,
Hold it tight,
Love me tomorrow
As you do this night,
Fill my dreams
As you might,
Lay here beside me
by tempered light,
wrap my heart
in scarlet ribbon,
fill it with joy,
let it be forgiven,
be my bedrock,
be my treasure,
render me a life,
brimming with pleasure
be my melody
and my song,
be with me
this life time long.

Tom Pheby

The Mansion

In the creepy mansion
On the very first floor
You hear a creak from the door
In the creepy mansion

You hear a scream
You hear a squawk
You start to run
Instead of walk
You hear footsteps
He's on your trail
Quickly hide
Or else you'll fail

In the creepy mansion
On the very first floor
You hear a creak from the door
In the creepy mansion

He's walked right passed you
Yes you've won!
Now here's your chance
Get out and run
Oh no, quick look out
Your last words
Were a scream and a shout?

Nikita Marshall

Be Raven Or Dove

She opens her eyes, she sees.
Yet she sees not the flowers, but dark fiery towers
and mist lingers around them
the devil confound them

She's open to sound she hears
but like the drop of a pin the sound in her ears
is lost in the din
from the heartbeat within

She hesitates then, as if to speak
the softest of touch, so tender so much
from beyond the clouds
a sunbeam unshrouds

She lowers her body, succumbs
like the change of a season, no particular reason
to fight or to love
be Raven or Dove.

Chimera my wife the love of my life
transforming a goddess, Chameleon modest
we now become one
our differences gone.

Martin Steven Colclough

Indeed

An event, when we were small
was a daring deed.
Balancing whilst walking on a wall,
or putting on a brave face if we should fall.
A caring deed was
a comforting arm round a friend
who's broken toy you promise to mend.
A sharing deed
when you offer your very last sweet,
or move up to allow more space on a seat.
A sparing deed is
pressing lightly with your crayoning stick,
or ensuring that your water colour is not too thick,
and a pairing deed
that special mate. A friend for life,
one day, maybe your husband or even your wife.

Christopher Smith

Struggle Within

I've just come in from the rain.
Watching the smoke that shouldn't have been
From the cigarette that I shouldn't have lit.
Thinking thoughts better left unsaid
And wishing things I don't deserve.
Standing melancholy as though to befit
This sentence I've hung over myself.
Twisting and turning to shrug off the blows,
The punches I throw and bruise within.
Poking and prodding till it over flows,
The confusion reigns like the smoky trail.
Watching it spread, infecting,
Thinning out in the air, but to no avail.
The smell does linger, like the pain.
It's wispy ghost does haunt to drive you insane.
Sifting through the painful and the complex
To simplify thought's that could only vex.
Whether you scream them out or achingly sigh
Or tumble over words that fall down to lie.
Awaiting you to kick and stir them up once more.
Slapping you in the face like you haven't felt them before.
The cold light of day has turned to a dusty haze.
There is no light left to capture my gaze.
Distorted you know the view to be,
But see anything else I would
If there was anything else to see.
Still I shake myself and say 'I deceive'.
Cause in some kind of hope I have to believe.

Jessica Warren

Wasted

For years, not just months, nor a schoolgirl crush of weeks
I gave you my life, it was wasted.
I am angry I wasted so much time on you,
and because I never once hesitated.
I am sad you won't see the things that I saw,
when I met your life and I became yours.
Together we conquered the world you and I,
but all of the time they were dreams in the sky.
Is it easier to hold the wind as it blows,
than to tell you the truth of my heart and my soul.
It was always for you and you cast me aside,
you dismissed me, but kept me, and always implied,
we would get there eventually, there would be an end,
but now I know I can't have you and I don't want a friend.
I took what little you gave me, I never complained,
safe in the knowledge that we'd 'be' again.
And on my journey of our dreams you never did mention,
that to ruin my faith was your only intention.
I'll forgive you for giving me those moments of bliss,
I'll forgive you for everything even for this.
I'll forgive you for saying you'll never be mine,
But I will never forgive you for wasting my time.

Cara Louise Thorner

Home Thoughts

When shadows of loneliness and of doubt,
Troubles within and troubles without
Blight our lives and break our heart,
And from happy times we are far apart
And nothing seems to offer us hope,
For our life is on a slippery slope,
We can find no comfort or relief,
Our life seems empty, filled with grief
And we feel so helpless, so alone,
Those are times we long for home

As we grow from child to man,
And play our role in life's great plan,
We live our life from day to day,
In times of work and times of play,
We see times of joy and times of pain,
Times of loss and times of gain,
What is to be we cannot know,
We let life lead us where we go
But no matter how far away we roam,
Our thoughts are never far from home

We may fall in love, and our life is a joy,
Which no troubles can ever destroy
Those are days when to us it seems,
We will fulfil all our hopes and dreams
But at other times we feel hurt and pain,
Happy times no longer remain
But even when we feel such an ache,
And our hearts seem about to break,
We need never face our troubles alone,
For we always find a way back home.

Trevor Spencer

TV Celebrity

Tempted to turn tempted to call
No deed just thought
My brother is what you are
You're rags you're hunger for all to see
you're famous and starving on TV

argue why and why we wont
help you now and why we can't
your innocence is left to die
no concern of ours
and said with pride

should you die within a week
you will be replaced
with countless more, who need and seek
ten pounds is all you ask
you've lost more around your cheeks
I'll sit here and sympathise
For that moment I'm in your life

but remember this and if you live
what guarantees can god give
that my donation will find its way
and assure my place on judgement day.

Mark Ritchie

An Ode To Wimborne

Oh! To be in Darset!
Now that spring is 'ere
But you must see my Wimborne
In its 13 hundredth year

This town with so much history
This town with its great charm
Is MY town I'm proud to say
So please do it no harm

Join us here to celebrate
These years of history,
Minster, Museum, Model Town
There is so much to see

To those who wish to change us
To you I send this plea
Leave us alone so we can keep
Our years of history

Sheila Hamlyn

Five Minutes At Tea Time

Sitting in my armchair
Reading the latest news
I glance at the T.V.
There was a man
One of the chosen few
An old gentleman sits in
His garden reliving his horrors of war
Recalling the death of his friends
A haunting memory that never ends
Pain and anguish etched on his face
I long to reach and comfort him and all
His sadness erase, a tear runs down
My face and blurs the print below
A sense of emptiness engulfs me as I
Listen to his thoughts of long ago
'Nana' booms my grandson's voice, startled
I rush to see, what catastrophe awaits me
He was only having his tea,
Standing by the table
Food and drink strewn all over the place
Guilt and apprehension all over his five your old face
'it wasn't me Nana are you very cross'
without a word I swept him up
and hugged him very tight,
don't worry pet I whispered
everything will be alright
he looked sheepishly into my eyes
then beamed a great big smile
I felt the love rise in my heart
And hugged him for quite a while.

Susan Evans

Dreams

Close your eyes
Drift off to sleep
Unravel you passions
Make mountainous leaps.
Here in your world of secrets you keep.
Taking flight like a bird
Above the treetops you weep.
Free from the fear that
Below follows me,
I've escaped from you now,
No more blood cannot seep
From the wounds you
Inflicted with your weapon so deep.

Janet Griffiths

My Dearest Love

To be with you is my desire,
forever and a day.
I love you more than life itself,
And this, I have to say…

If you should ever leave me pet,
no matter what the cause.
I could not face the world again,
for life would reach a pause.

Where all the joy and sun had fled,
and dark despair remains.
And icy winds blow o'er the earth,
where lies my heart in chains.

Without your love, I could not be,
the person that I am.
You are the inspiration sweet,
that maketh me a man!

A man to live, a man to fight,
to keep you from all harm.
And make for you, in this troubled world,
a place of peace and calm!

Christopher James West

Blue Star Line

Packed my bag, caught the train
Ready for my first trip
Made our way to Princess dock to sail on my first ship
Swear I saw a worried look in my father's eye
He knew he'd lost his little boy as we waved goodbye.

We headed down the Mersey cross the Irish sea
My new life had just begun but it was new to me
Just when I felt all alone a voice said 'you'll be fine'
Me and Mickey standing aft
On the blue star line.

We sailed across the ocean and the seven seas
We were young and free then and did as we pleased
Cruisin' with my shipmates drinking with the girls
Me and Mickey in every bar
All around the world.

Letters came every day from my girl back home
Having fun I didn't care she was all alone
Girls would flock around the ship at the red ensign
Why'da need a girl back home
When you're on the Blue star line.

Many times we'd sit at night watching ships go by
Wanderin' if their watching us out of telescopic eyes
Now many ships I sailed upon
Crossed many a maidens door
The world was so much bigger then many a sight I'd saw.

But it was good to be back home suntanned rich and free
To see my father standing there waiting on the quay
Now I'm older and settled down things have crossed my mind
What great times that we had
On the Blue star line.

Alan Unsworth

How Different Life Could Be

There's no justice in this world,
No justice I can see,
We work our fingers to the bone
And give our love for free,
Yet when the worm decides to turn
It does so with such spite,
It sucks the life force from our souls
And bleeds our will to fight.

There's no reason for this pain,
No reason I can see,
If we work together to an end
How different life could be,
Then if the worm should try to turn
It finds our fears are few,
And shies away from our resolve
That's steadfast, strong and true.

Graham Allaway

Clocking In

Clocking in for work, and in and out of bed
the ringing of the alarm clock is what I really dread,
One eye open, one eye closed, I hop around the floor
Trying to find all the things I dropped the night before,
Searching round the bedroom for my clothes I forage
I stumble down the stairs and have my bowl of porridge.

The day has not yet started, and I'm wishing it would end
just the thought of my dull job, it drives me round the bend,
I'm ready now to start the day, I close the door behind
to begin another working day of boring monotonous grind.

Ding goes the clock and now it all begins
the banging and the clanging, that bloody awful din,
Roll on 12 o clock so I can stop for lunch
All the lads I work with are such a happy bunch,
Ribbing one another, a joke shared here and there
Without our constant banter, would leave me in despair,
Sharing fun and laughter helps me through the day
Oh how I wish for 5 o clock I wish my life away.

Oh God, please hurry up the day begins to drag
the foreman's on my shoulder he always seems to nag,
clocking in and clocking off is all I seem to do
I can't wait for 5 o clock my working day is through.

Pushing and shoving everywhere, to get outside the door
how great it is to leave that noisy factory floor,
Oh to win the lottery, just a little win
just enough so I don't have to face that daily din,
no more clocking in and out, oh what joy it brings
that I don't have to plan my day, around those bleeding dings.

One more thing I like to do, the thought makes my heart throb
To see the foreman one more time, to punch him in the gob,
Its only wishful thinking, which only dreams can bring
To wake up every morning, without that bloody ding.

Mary L Murray

Sorry?
(for the providers of inspiration)

A hasty plaster,
Just a word,
A quick fix,
A lie.
Scantily applied
Without meaning
Or care.

You shoddy 'apology',
It's unfelt,
Unneeded,
Barely acknowledged.
You abuse the word
It's an excuse-
Turning your back to Responsibility

As if the very utterance;
Makes the sun shine,
Halts earthquakes,
Lifts one lazy finger.
The sardonic smile
Sneers at the genuine,
Falsities over ride them.

Lucy Quarrier

The Butterfly

I once felt inside like a butterfly,
with wings flying high.
Beautiful and bright.
Not a worry in sight.

Now I feel deep inside
like a butterfly...
But one who can't fly,
cause it has no wings.

A butterfly is a butterfly,
inside and out.
But what is a butterfly
without its wings?

Its ugly and sad.
A blog of existence.
Unable and to move,
unable to change.

Hopeless,
Desperate,
Unable to fly.
Just sat there staring at the world.
Asking for some help,
as the time passes by.

Changed from a Caterpillar
into a cocoon.
Then to a butterfly.
Now into doom

Would you help that butterfly
or walk on by?
Cause soon the butterfly will die,
if its no longer able to fly.

Karen Winch

On The Wolds

Oh to walk on the Wolds with you,
Beautiful views and skies of blue.
A good pair of legs and a strong heart,
You will enjoy this ramble from the start.

Rambling hill and deep lush valley,
Gurgling streams where we can tarry.
Newborn lambs and woolly sheep,
Never far from their bleat.

Waving green sea of winter wheat
Pretty village with a welcome seat.
Wonderful trees stately and tall,
Marvellous colours in the fall.

A skylark singing up above,
The gentle cooing of a dove.
Wild flowers too numerous to name,
Plenty of colourful strutting game.

Hares, rabbits, deers and foxes,
Hide and play in green copses.
Look around its all for free,
God made it all for you and me.

Kath Staves

Bluebells

Bluebells in the woods so bright
Shimmering in the sun of light
Flowing in the wind so fair
Raindrops trickling in my hair
Bells are ringing turn out a light
Bluebells in the woods 'Goodnight'.

J Clark

Fragrance Free

Clever words
can be likened to flowers.
The worst of them
send sharp signals
to assault the primitive brain,
while the best
have an allure
unsupported by base senses;
whisper softly,
'look at me,
I am beautiful.'

Tina Bass

Shades Of Gray

Shades of gray and darkening skies,
Deep searching looks from empty eyes.
No hope of a future not even a gleam,
Not a ray of sunshine to be seen.

Long dark roads that go on for miles.
No sounds of laughter or even smiles.
Just long dark days that came and went
To add to your feelings of discontent.

Deep dark depressions with clouds of despair
That appears to follow you everywhere.
Large open spaces with deep dark voids,
Echoes of loneliness leaving a chilling noise.

Sounds in the distance way back in your mind,
Desperately trying to recall a time
Of music and laughter from way back when.
Will I ever recapture those days again?

Graham Smith

Your Common Or Garden Slug

It's rotten being a slug,
Bombarded with salt all the time;
Wherever we go, no matter how slow,
We're covered all over with lime.

Then there's eggshells, of course, lacerations we feel,
And it really is rough on the tummy;
We can't turn to you, so what else can we do?
But suffer and crawl home to Mummy.

Adopted as PETS - (there's not been one yet)
It appears that you're all in a muddle,
Your cats, dogs and rabbits are petted and kissed, and
WE don't get even a cuddle.

We never get fed or have treats 'on the side'
Would you like this to happen to you?
No! You don't care, as you look in despair,
You just stamp on us - with your shoe.

Slug pellets are cruel, but we eat them all,
(Can I make just a simple suggestion?)
As we look back at you, ugly faces we view,
It's enough to give one indigestion.

So, if you wish to live and thrive,
You let a spider run alive:
Don't think of us as ugly bugs,
But common or garden 'victimised' slugs.

Pam Cope

Escape

How is it possible? She had forgotten.
A few short hours ago she was on her bike
pumping coursing thrumming on a country road
with yellow rapeseed lighting up patches
of green hills, tangled weeds, crazy wild spring
like a jazz song, all improvisation and descants and
surprises. The sky was unfolded like soft blue cotton
and her blood was humming and her face felt
fresh-crisp in the chilled breeze.
But then the words came when she was home,
the written words of rejection,
and there was no wind and no wild and
it ate her insides out, carved out a spot where
her heart once was as if Pain was now the
puppet master and she twitched on the
strings of nothingness.
So she curled into herself, wrapped tight
and buried in, deep and deeper still, and struggled
to find new words, new ways of finding again
that ride, that air - the open spaces
in the world and in her mind where for a moment
(if only that) it no longer hurt.

Kaleen Love

Bullies

Would, that I could
Cover my ears
And hear
No more the taunts and jeers.
Nor tremble when they hiss and sneer
An elbow dig, then twist the wrist
Threatened with a balled up fist.
'If one world of this you utter,
More of this we'll make you suffer!'
Why should I dread
The days ahead.
They see the bruises
Make excuses
Just high spirits, kidding around
Don't make a fuss
It could be worse.
And so, dismissed
Defeated
I retreated.

Jean MacGregor

The Elastic Defeatist

relentlessly disbelieve
as soon as tremors wither in quite,
frightful hoax for the fate soaked mute
potent thoughts penetrate his punctured middle
 His hard humour takes infinite durations to digest,
what else is new? But for some insight to purpose,
would he not readily barter flesh or stone,
when kind efforts in earnest inherit
untold favour-scented scorn.
pray for patience.

Nathan Haridien

The Charmer

Alone,
Play it cool
Charm the birds from the trees
You'd have to be a charmer to get past that hair.
Disaster,
Embarrassment,
Obsession,
Disbelief,
How could you take that from me,
Meet her
And then try to disappear?
How foolish I was to try and follow you,
How vain,
How crushed
When I finally knew what it was.

Joanne Levey

The Inhabitant

You are my ghost
When I only can think of you
While you are away;
I am your phantom,
When I am gone out totally of your life,
And I only left just a little, a little,
Tinge of disturbances in you,
Which will haunt you unexpectedly from afar,
When my inhabitancy in your body
Has been deranged.

T Lau

Age Of Reason

Forty years old
No it cannot be
I'm so full of life
I am thirty three.

Half a century
The sakes alive!
I can't be fifty
I'm forty five.

I'm never sixty
I feel so nifty
Still got my teeth
I'm only fifty.

Seventy is so very sad
And I am full of fun
So come what may
I'll just be sixty one.

Even though they've all been told.
They won't believe that I am old
Unbelieving, jokey and matey
I have to insist that I am eighty.

Betty Robinson

Love At First Sight

The very first time I looked at him,
It make my heart beat fast
I fell in love completely-
I knew that it would last
He didn't really notice me,
He didn't even smile
But I just stared so lovingly
Gazing at him for a while
He turned his head and looked away
He didn't even know
That I had given him my heart
And that I loved him so,
Just one glace it took,
To set my heart ablaze
This love for him will last
To the end of all my days
How powerful is the gift of love
To happen as quickly as this
I hadn't even held his hand
Much less a loving kiss
But as time goes on, this love of mine
I hope will love me too,
I have a faint suspicion
That is what he'll do
But just in case you are wondering
Who has changed my life so far
Well, he's my little grandson-
And I'm his proud grandma.

Marjorie Corrie

A Tree

I think I'd like to be a tree
Standing still all day
Chatting to the birds and bees
Until they fly away.

I would like to stand in a shady lane
With a babbling brook close by
Cowslips primroses violets blue
And the sun shining in the sky.

Looking down from such a height
On all the things below
Watching while small creatures play
And the children who come and go.

When the wind blows cold and my branches are bare
I'll think of God and the spring,
That he'd send me new shoots
And once again, the birds will forever sing.

Please don't cut the trees down,
They are gifts from God above,
Planted so many years ago
And looked on by all with love.

Muriel Bowles

Musical Thoughts

Sweet music to my ears,
That brings me to tears,
As I remember through the years,
All my thoughts and fears,
Upon my conscience deeply sears,
The memories of all those jeers,
The feel of misguided leers,
From my so called peers,
Who called me one of their dears,
As the truth upon me nears,
As reality's ugly head rears,
I AM THE ONLY ONE WHO HEARS!

Peter Jones

The Treacherous Floods

No one can imagine the horrors of a flood,
Creeping very ominously-it really chills the blood,
Creating a mass of mud as a slimy treacherous hell,
Made up of alien sludge that exudes a foul smell.

Some victims suffer illness as well as utter loss
Of many prized possessions some difficult to cost,
Swept away or ruined, it's hard for them to face
That many of their treasures will never be replaced.

When the flood at last subsides it gives a brief respite,
Though many of its victims no longer sleep at night,
There's many anxious hours after all the wind and rain,
Fearing almost constantly the floods come yet again.

Spare a thought for all the folk who suffer in this way,
Trying hard to celebrate some joy on Christmas day,
Most of them experience some sleepless nights of fear
Or wonder what fate may deal in the promising New Year.

Tom Tucker

Could You?

Could you catch my tears?
I'd love to see you try.
Could you ease my fears?
You'd never stop me cry.
Could you hold my hand?
I know that you'd let go.
Could you even understand?
It's something I don't know.
For all my life I've always dreamt
I thought I'd touch the sky, I meant
To dream and live and love and fly,
The skies were mine, I'd never cry.
My tears they fall and like the rain
When tomorrow comes they fall again.
I can't explain this and I don't know why
Could you be the one to stop me cry?

Clare Hyland

Our Mam

You protected us when we were young
You were always around when things went wrong
You never complained when things were rough
You would say never mind it will make us tough
You taught us patience, wisdom, honesty and to be kind
And always try to be dignified
You were a force to behold
With a heart of gold
Our lives are now hollow
What an act to follow
Never take your Mam for granted for the job she does
She will do it with a heart full of love
So love your mother all you can
While you have her now
You will not have her all your life
Believe me now nothing can compare
With the disbelief and despair
When you open your eyes each day
And your Mam is not there.

Marie Elliott

The Future

The young ones living in our town will rule the town tomorrow,
So teach them now the way to live with joy, and not with sorrow.
Teach them to put their trust in God, their worries with him share,
Help put strong faith into their hearts 'the Lord God's always there.
Then when they are grown, and run the town,
with peace and love for all,
Their faith will stand up firm and strong, their trust will never fall.
With God to help them every day, they'll keep the town on its feet,
Their children will be safe at night to walk along any street.
Each one will love their neighbour, and have Christian girls and boys,
To fill the town with happiness, by sharing all their joys.
So don't neglect the children, hear what they have to say,
Help them in any way that you can to live their life the happy way.
Then when you're old and they rule the town,
they'll rule it with true love,
Learnt from the help you gave them, and also from God above.

Nita Garlinge

Learning

What is this life?

Five decades one worships the economy
The Earth revolving, its imaginary 'axis' rooted beneath a pound sign.

Why must I balance upon a rickety old stool,
only finding that if my hands chose to roam,
I discover hardened gum smothered in a pleasant coating of foreign,
stale saliva under this lab desk,
As I listen to the squeak and drone of the authority ahead?
Assuming they know best.
Assuming I don't already know.

Why must one, from the age of 4,
spend their life assuming an ambition?
Why must we have dreams?
Can we not wallow if we so wish?

What do I wish of this mammoth world?
My insignificance overwhelms me.

Am I lost or do I complain for what I don't realise I yearn?
Do I despise this institute of phoney respect
Or am I comforted by its friendly washed-out green walls?

I may seem young, feelings erratic, however I must admit this.
For there is no chance I could believe that ignorance is bliss.

Laura Collopy

The Best Time Of The Day

The best time of the day
When the wheel has come to rest
The day extracted its' measure
To her treasury chest
The subtle invasion vanished
The chit chatter ceased
Then darkness' companion flickers
The flame of his short lease

And love will come to find you
To lay his head in place
And dwell in the softness
Of lovers' warm embrace
And there two souls will mingle
Among the secret quiet hours
Until at last they journey
Through the time that sleep devours

Adrian Green

Butterfly

Fresh from its chrysalis,
Part of a summer's day,
A vision of colour and grace,
A butterfly floating by.

Fragile and so beautiful,
Sailing in the breeze,
The most delicate of insects,
A butterfly floating by.

Carried high and far,
Without care and thought,
A symbol of freedom,
A butterfly floating by.

Chris Brown

Lonely Soul

I'm a lonely soul of unwanted love
as she took the beats away from my heart
She gave me feelings I never felt
as a man only to tear them apart
I took to her like a bird to the sky
as we shared our days of pain
This lonely soul has loved his last,
he will never give his love the same
A lonely soul I am and I suffer to this very day
But I can't help but say thank you
to the girl who chased my heart away
To thank her because I realised that
she was too young to receive my love
My heart was too mature for her
and now it's her who's stuck
She phoned for me to take her back
but now she's on her own
I may have loved her once before
but I have another lonely soul
This time she gives me comfort
she holds me when I'm down
She makes me feel like sunshine
whenever she's around
I think its love I feel
but then I'm not to sure
I don't feel anything like the way I felt before
But one feeling that I do know is
that she feels very strong for me
I will give her all my effort
and in the future we will see
So for now this soul has finished
and would like to say goodbye
Goodbye to being lonely
and for being happy when I die.

Ben Growden

Chain Reaction

I looked upon my daughter with tenderness and pride,
It only seemed like yesterday that she became a bride,
I glanced upon my handsome son,
And recalled with joy when his life begun,
I am part of life's rich tapestry,
Of ups and downs and travesty,
A Mum.

Life's cycle is still spinning,
And each day a new life is beginning,
With hopes and dreams and heartfelt joy,
My daughter has a little boy,
I am part of life's rich tapestry,
Of ups and downs and travesty,
A Gran.

Just a link in a huge chain,
Which is always changing, never the same,
Let's seize the moment and celebrate,
Yes, life can be hell but sometimes first rate.
I am part of life's rich tapestry,
Of ups and downs and travesty,
An OAP.

Barbara Ryder

Monet's Wife

Today with him I am spell bounded, enchanted by his
lighter shades of pinks, reds and greens
And the slow rhythmic movement of his hands
Forming lines, curves on a white canvas, empty and lonely
I am the blank canvas - waiting to be filled -
with inks, waters and distorted colours
Unusual blurs and reflections in the water
My beloved's paintbrush dipped in a palette
of a sea of paint,
I imagined his kisses like coloured gems
dropping down on my cheeks
the coloured gems were second in line
after his moments
in gardens…
with other women…
which he stared at for hours and hours
I longed to be loved, to be treasured like his art
Just to be looked at by his eyes
As I rocked myself to sleep -
and held my broken heart,
His eyes were focused on a curved, Japanese bridge
At the garden of Giverny.

Selina Mirpuri

A Natural Soldier

His mother was buried
without a dirge;
on her were laid the
petals of allied-bombing.

What mine is exploding
beneath the black wheels of his stare?
Nothing survived
the occupying forces.

Next year
he will lay a rifle lovingly
like the stalk of carnation that
blooms
when nature squeezes its bud.

Colin Gerard Tan

The Butterfly Keeper

They hit me like a runaway train,
Butterfly's the size of dragonflies,
From deep down inside me they took flight,
Tinkling my inner being,
Sending shock waves through my body.

I held my chest tight for fear they would escape,
They felt good inside me,
Exciting, their wings vibrating,
Sending more shock waves through my body.

Laugh at me if you must Mr Butterfly Keeper,
This is your doing,
Only you can make the butterflies take flight,
Like today, when I heard your warm captivating voice on the phone.
You are the butterfly keeper,
You, hold the key to the door of the butterfly house...

Janette Vatcher